Guide to
INDIGENOUS
ARTIFACTS
of the Northeast

Roger W. Moeller, Ph.D.
Director of Research
American Indian Archaeological Institute
Washington, CT

Hancock House

ISBN-13: 978-0-88839-295-4

Editor Elizabeth McLenehan
Typeset by Lisa Smedman in Times Roman on an AM Varityper Comp/ Edit
Production & Layout Crystal Ryan
Cover Design Peter Burakoff
Photos Roger Moeller and Alice Kitselman
Harpoon Illustration by Jean Pruchnik
Printed in Canada by Friesen Printers

Hancock House gratefully acknowledges the Semiahmoo, Kwantlen and Katzie First Nations, whose unceded traditional territories our offices reside upon.

Hancock House
Hancock House Publishers Ltd.
19313 Zero Avenue, Surrey, B.C., Canada V3Z 9R9
Hancock House Publishers
Unit #104-4550 Birch Bay Lynden Rd, Blaine, WA 98230
(800)-938-1114   sales@hancockhouse.com   hancockhouse.com

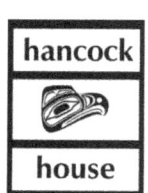

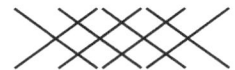

TABLE OF CONTENTS

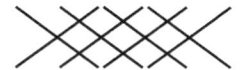

INTRODUCTION

The Indigenous peoples who once inhabited New England as long as 10,000 years ago left behind many artifacts that are of particular interest to the archaeologist studying early Indigenous culture. A careful examination of the remnants that have been excavated in this region provides an insight into the activities and development of the native inhabitants of North America. Artifacts such as tools and utensils indicate a routine of subsistence pursuits: fishing, hunting, and gathering; food preparation and storage; and tool manufacture. Other articles offer some clues to the nature of the religion and aesthetics of the early Indigenous culture.

In order to achieve a better understanding of prehistoric Indigenous cultures, archaeologists must examine the original documents written by firsthand observers. Early traders, explorers, missionaries, and travelers to North America told of the strange customs of the Native Americans; however, some of their stories were deceptive, self-serving, and, in some instances, total fabrications. Consequently, archaeologists cannot rely solely on written historical records in determining the nature of prehistoric Indigenous cultures. Rather they must use the written material to supplement their excavations.

Today, archaeologists are using more sophisticated research techniques in excavating early Indigenous sites. By studying artifacts in relation to the carbonized plants, seeds, charcoal, bones, pollen, and soils found in association with them, scientists are able to identify more accurately the environmental context of the pieces, the approximate dates, and the seasons in which specific areas were occupied. This method of examining and identifying the artifacts helps archaeologists determine the history of the first inhabitants of New England.

Most of the artifacts pictured were collected many decades ago. Because they were found in a context that made dating difficult, they have been assigned approximate ages, based on information from adjacent excavation sites where dates were available. Many common items in the Indigenous person's tool kit, such as knives and scrapers, retained the same form as when they were first invented. Other items, such as projectile points and pottery, were subject to a great deal of change through time. Since wood, bone, hide, and fiber decay so rapidly in the New England soil, only the most recent sites have provided evidence of items made from these materials.

The artifacts have been grouped according to their known or suspected function. Many artifacts, particularly tools, exhibit characteristic wear patterns that help determine their use. Others have uses that can be identified because of their similarity to implements still in use today. However, some items had functions that cannot be determined outside of their original cultural context. Had the birdstone only been found in association with the objects the people used with it, we might have a clue to its original purpose. The same is true of artifacts such as the bannerstone and plummet. Out of context, the objects become merely well-made, decorative enigmas.

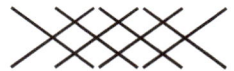

SUBSISTENCE PURSUITS

Hunting with spears, javelins, and, later, arrows was widely practiced in New England. Probably the most abundant artifact in any collection is the projectile point. Those pictured represent more than 10,000 years in the development of Indigenous hunting weaponry. Styles changed slowly through time. Most of the projectile points that have been preserved are of stone, but many were also made of bone. Another hunting implement was the bola, which is still in use today on the pampas of Argentina. The ends of three hide thongs were securely fastened to individual bola stones and then the free ends were tied together. The hunter twirled the weapon above his head and threw it at his prey to entrap the animal's legs.

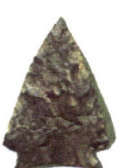 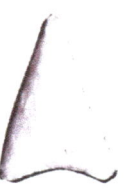 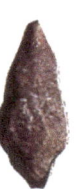 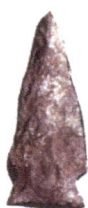

Because the bow and arrow was a relatively recent invention, not all projectile points are arrowheads. Some were for javelins or spears.

 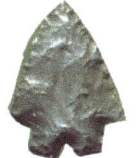 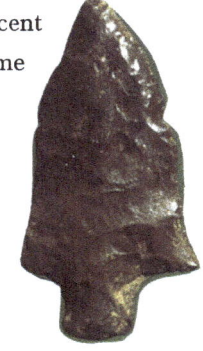

Stone was not the only raw material for projectile points. These are made of bone.

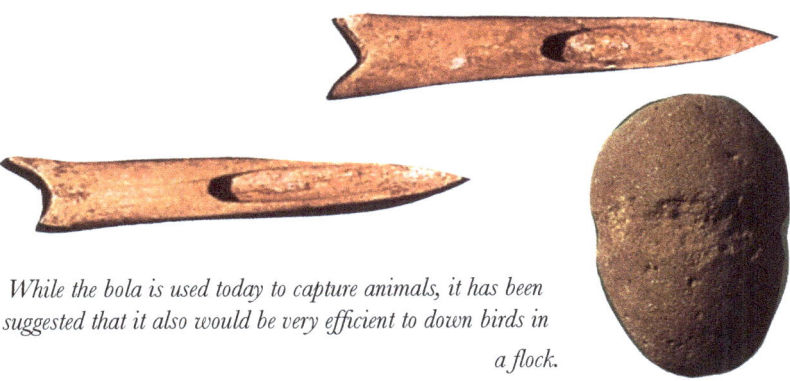

While the bola is used today to capture animals, it has been suggested that it also would be very efficient to down birds in a flock.

Fishing is another well-documented activity of prehistoric times. Woven nets made from twisted plant fibers were weighted with crudely notched pebbles found along the ocean shore or stream banks. These may have been used as casting nets, stationary seines, or drag nets, depending upon the number of people available, the types of fish, and the nature of the waterway. Hooks, which were made by cutting bones or by lashing hawthorn barbs to sticks, were less efficient for catching large numbers of fish, but they could have been used in great quantities for unattended lines.

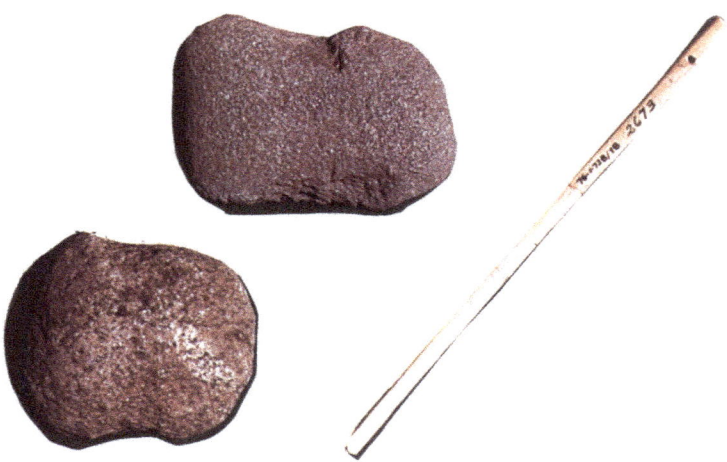

Netsinkers (left) come in a wide variety of sizes and weights. Most are very crudely notched. This net weaver (right) was made by cutting an animal rib.

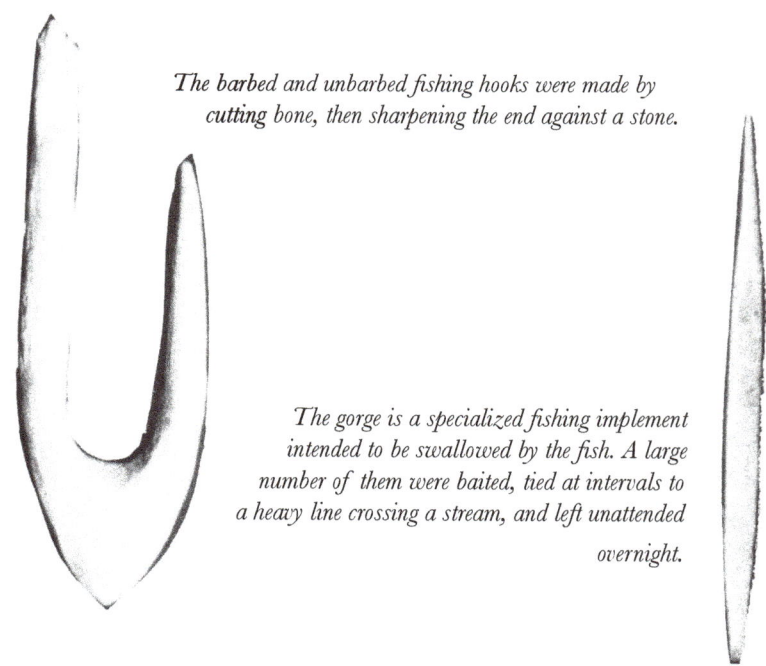

The barbed and unbarbed fishing hooks were made by cutting bone, then sharpening the end against a stone.

The gorge is a specialized fishing implement intended to be swallowed by the fish. A large number of them were baited, tied at intervals to a heavy line crossing a stream, and left unattended overnight.

Harpoons were used to spear very large fish or, more frequently, aquatic animals such as seals, walrus, and otters. The harpoon had a line attached to a detachable head. As the barb was driven into the soft flesh, the spear detached and the animal was hauled in by the line.

Although fishing and hunting provided the bulk of the food, the Indigenous people could not always depend on procuring large game every day. Consequently, it was essential to gather shellfish, berries, seeds, nuts, and slow-moving game to supplement their diet.

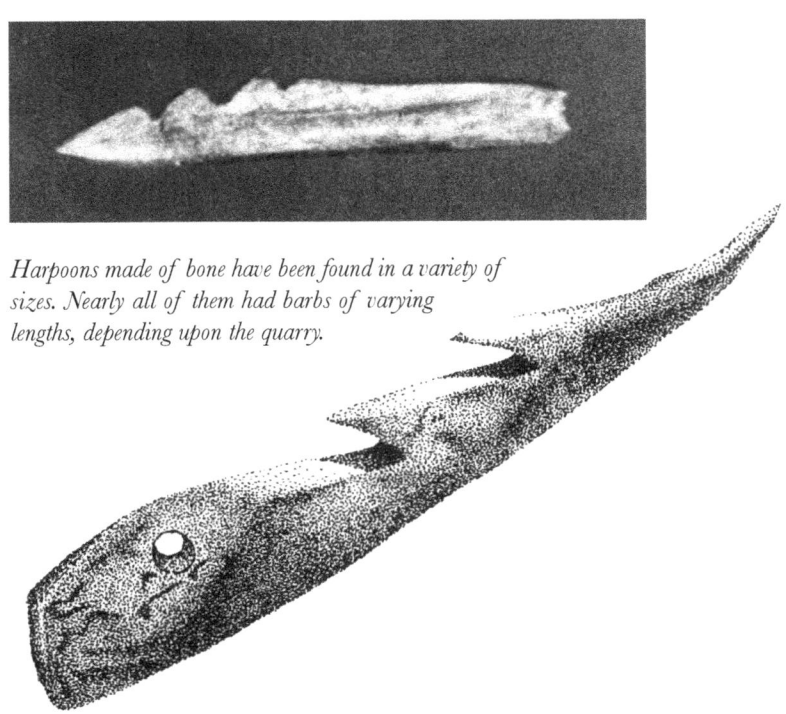

Harpoons made of bone have been found in a variety of sizes. Nearly all of them had barbs of varying lengths, depending upon the quarry.

Baskets and a variety of containers made from bark and hide were used for food gathering. Very few examples have survived, however, since organic materials do not preserve well and also because of the later development of clay pottery vessels, which, once fired, were not perishable. Consequently, archaeologists must depend upon processing tools, rather than containers, to provide evidence of the importance and diversity of food gathering in early Indigenous culture.

The basic food-processing implement was the hammerstone , a simple tool used for crushing, grinding, and splitting seeds, nuts, and bones. Its lack of sophistication may explain why hammerstones appear in so many different forms. They vary from smooth to deeply pitted, symmetrical to shapeless, and dense to porous.

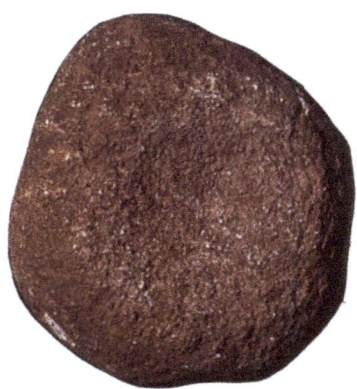

Hammerstones develop their characteristics through use. The pit is a result of use as an anvil.

Repeated battering rounds the edges to create the discoidal shape.

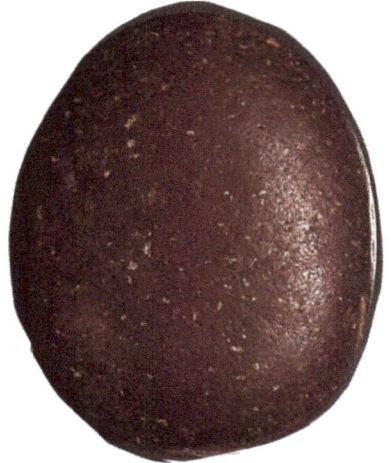

Mullers are worn smooth on the faces by grinding. Some, no doubt, doubled as hammerstones, as evidenced by their battered edges.

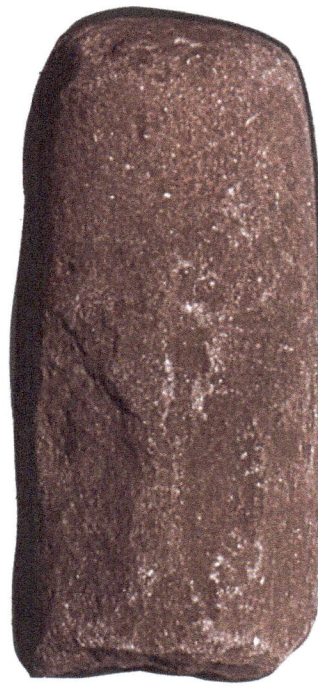

Pestles become increasingly cylindrical through use. The ends are frequently battered from crushing food in a stone bowl or mortar.

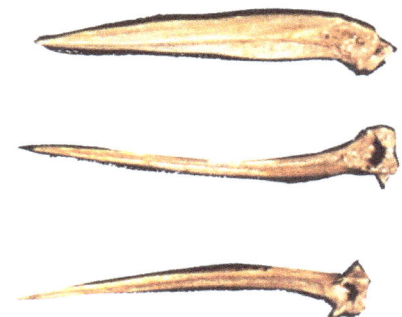

These skewers are sharpened drumfish spines.

The pestle, which was used to grind seeds to a fine consistency, usually became highly polished through constant use. Fragments of stone from the tool frequently mixed with the food and made a very gritty combination that caused dental problems over time.

Food was cooked by boiling, roasting, or broiling. A container filled with stew was often warmed by dropping in rocks heated over an open fire. This method of heating food was used when a container made of a flammable material, such as bark, could not be placed directly over the roaring fire. Seeds were quickly roasted by mixing them with hot coals spread onto a dish woven from plant fibers. Meat was cooked directly over the fire or on a spit. Small cups made of turtle shells may have been used to hold cooked food, and skewers may have been used to eat it.

The axe and celt were used to cut down trees and to roughly shape wooden objects. The gouge was a carving tool similar to the modern chisel, but it was used to remove larger amounts of wood. Unfortunately almost all of the wooden objects from the pre-Contact period have decayed without a trace.

Celts and axes were made by pecking a stone with another one to make the basic shape. The edge was then ground with a different stone. The bit was sharpened or polished by abrasion with a very fine-grained stone.

Axes differ from celts in that axes are grooved for hafting.

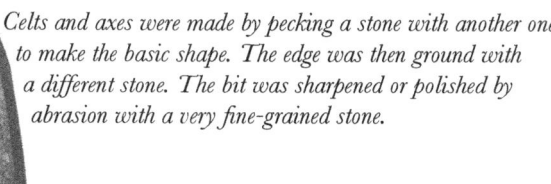

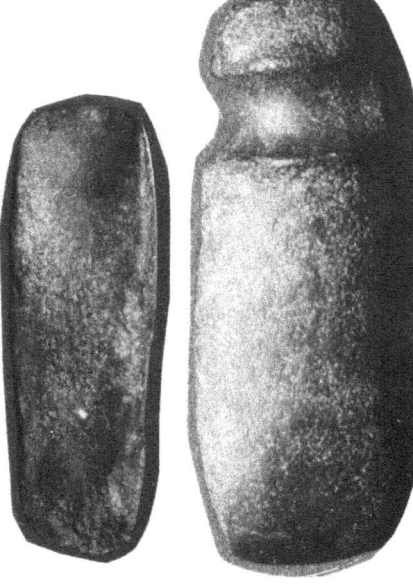

Gouges were manufactured in the same manner as axes and celts. The channel permits greater sharpening for closer cutting.

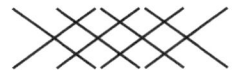

CEREMONIAL OBJECTS

The most difficult artifacts to interpret are those which the archaeologist has classified as decorative, ornamental, ceremonial, or religious. These objects present a mystery since they exhibit no evidence of a specific kind of use and are not clearly associated with other tools. Some of these may well have been designed to serve religious or political functions or to denote social rank, while others perhaps had no specific function other than as ornaments.

The bannerstone has a hole drilled through the center by a fire-hardened hollow reed. A slurry of fine sand and water provided sufficient abrasion for drilling.

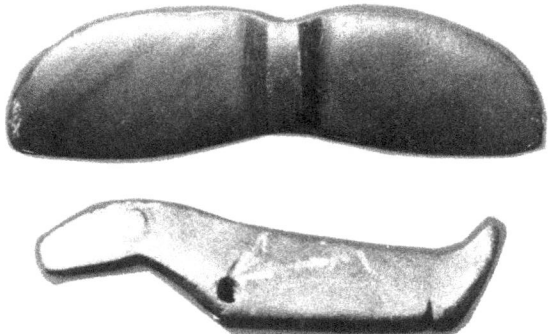

The birdstone was made by the very careful grinding and polishing of slate. Typically very high-quality stone was used.

The bannerstone and birdstone have frequently been called spear-thrower weights. When the stones were lashed to the spear thrower, the extra weight supposedly increased the hitting force of the spear. However, it is curious that they should be so well made, exhibit so little wear or damage, and be found in graves in association with other decorative, "ritual" items. It is possible that these unusual stones were the tokens of a particular band or social class or were symbols of political authority.

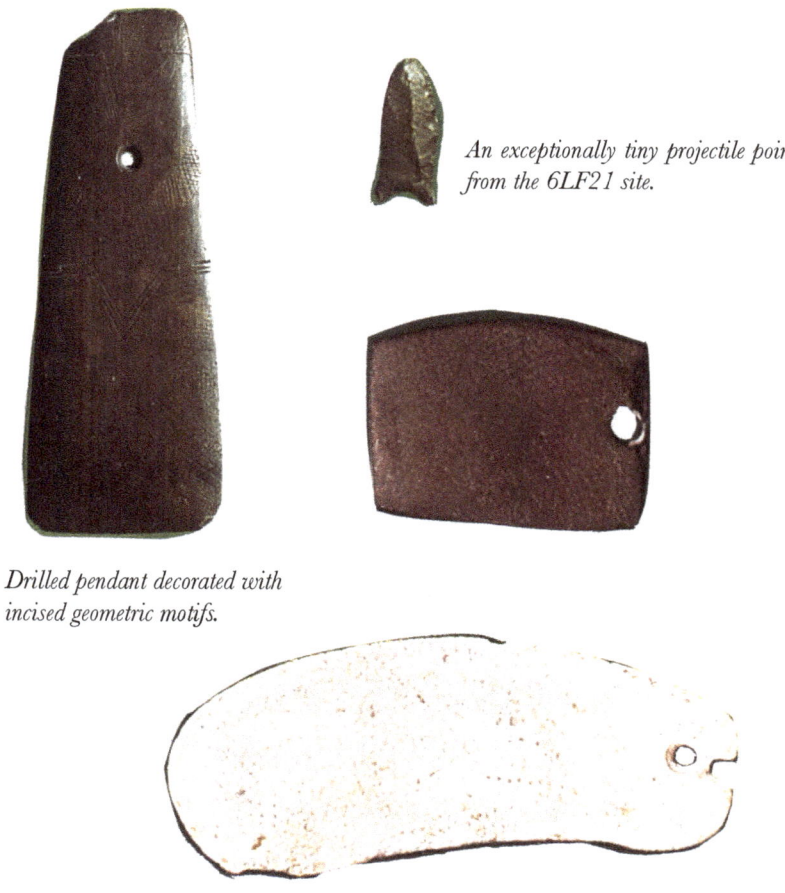

An exceptionally tiny projectile point from the 6LF21 site.

Drilled pendant decorated with incised geometric motifs.

Pendants were made in a variety of shapes and sizes. While stone is common, those made of shell and bone are found in more recent contexts.

The miniature points found at a 10,000-year-old site in Connecticut may also be classified as symbolic. Although these points are smaller versions of the larger fluted point found at the same site, they were not used in the same way as other projectile points. They may have been a form of charm carried to bring good luck in the hunt.

Pendants and beads of bone, shell, and polished stone have been used as ornaments in most societies, and it is probably safe to assume that the Indigenous peoples of prehistoric New England used them for decorative purposes, too. The finest pieces were probably worn by wealthier or higher-ranking members of the community.

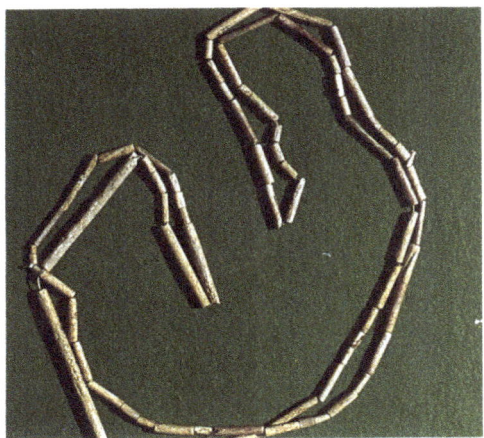

Individual beads were cut from bird bones, which are hollow.

Fish vertebrae were drilled through the center to make beads.

A soapstone bead, ring, or perforated disk was made by cutting, drilling, and polishing the very soft stone.

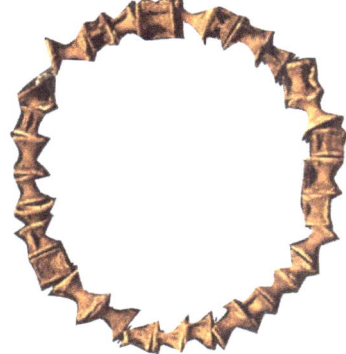

The smoking pipe featured strongly in religious ceremonies, rituals, and council meetings and was not, therefore, an object for casually passing the time. The cultivation and use of tobacco were highly regarded.

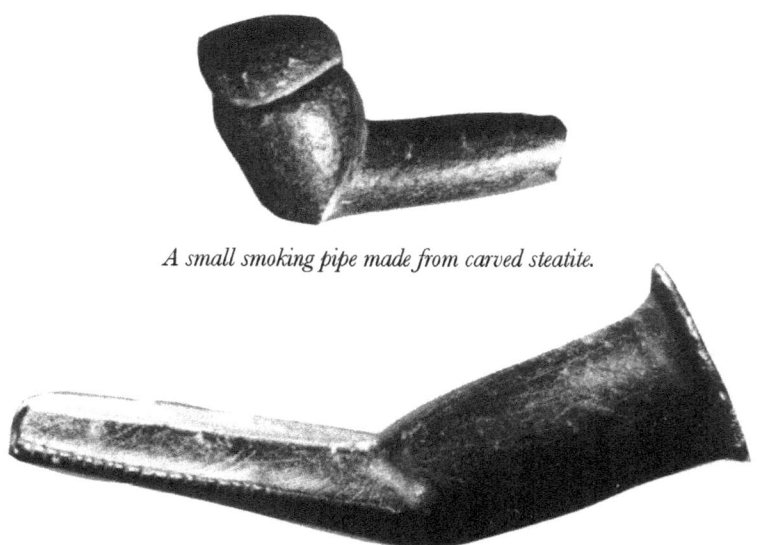

A small smoking pipe made from carved steatite.

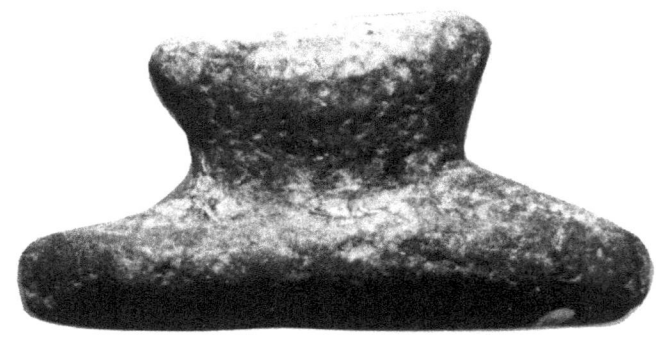

Pipe styles changed through time and became more ornate. This is carved from steatite and polished.

This is a steatite pipe in the process of manufacture. It will have a centrally placed bowl, rather than one at the end of the stem.

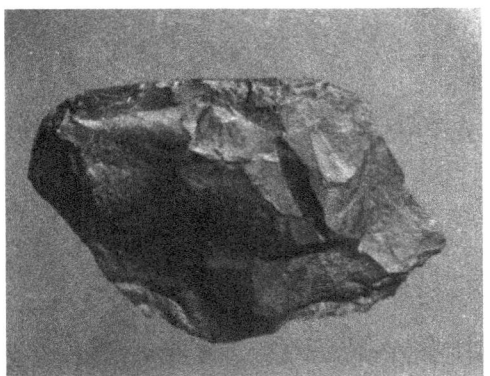

The weathered surface (cortex) has been removed by a hammerstone. The deep flake scars show the crude roughing-out of the core prior to more precise chipping.

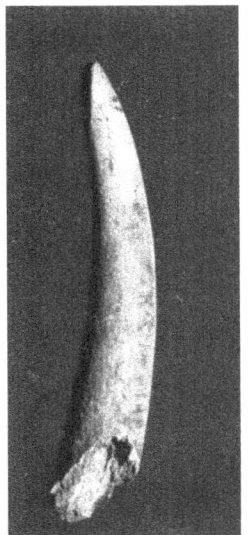

Antler flakers were used to carefully shape and sharpen stone projectile points, knives, drills, and scrapers.

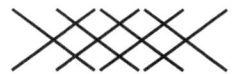

TOOLS

One of the most fascinating skills of prehistoric craftsmen was the manufacture of stone implements, such as projectile points, knives, drills, and scrapers. Making stone tools involved a careful selection of a core or basic chunk of stone on which work was begun, in order to avoid obvious flaws that would make it unworkable. The rough shape given the core by the initial chipping was determined by whether the finished tool was to be used for piercing, cutting, drilling, or scraping. To shape a projectile point or blade, the flintknapper used a hammerstone to remove large flakes from the core. A deer antler or hard wooden baton was then used to strike off successively smaller flakes in a regular, symmetrical pattern. The final stage of manufacture involved a process known as pressure flaking. Using an antler tine, pressure was applied to a small area and a twist of the wrist caused tiny flakes to chip off the opposite face.

The fluted point was so named for the shallow groove or flute on the blade. This groove thinned the blade to facilitate hafting to a wooden shaft.

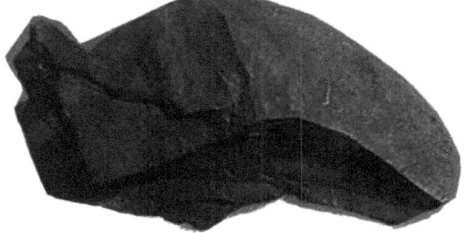

This knife was meant to be hand-held, not hafted.

The edges of the scraper have been very carefully flaked and have developed a polish because of use. This indicates it was used to scrape soft materials.

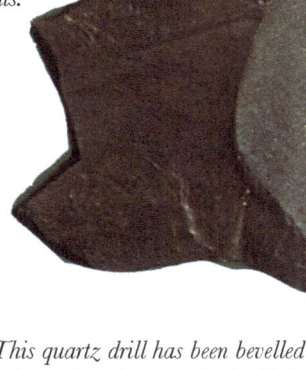

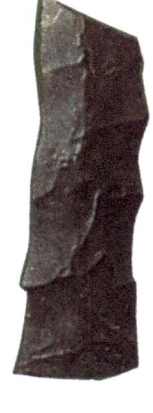

Channel flakes were struck from the center of the blade of the fluted point.

This quartz drill has been bevelled on the cutting edges to twist itself into the wood in the same way that a modern twist drill does. The tip was broken off during use.

Fluted points can be distinguished from other points because a channel flake has been removed to leave a groove. These points were used specifically for big-game hunting. One can recognize the characteristic channel flake as easily as the fluted point itself.

Knives, drills, and scrapers were made using the flaking process. Each tool had a uniquely fashioned cutting edge that was designed for particular tasks. These tools can be identified not only by their outlines, but also, more specifically, by the type of damage seen on the functional edges. The cutting of hides, wood, or plant fibers, drilling into hard or soft wood, and the scraping of hides, wood, or bone each leave distinctive wear patterns. This is a result of both the direction of use and the material the tool was used upon.

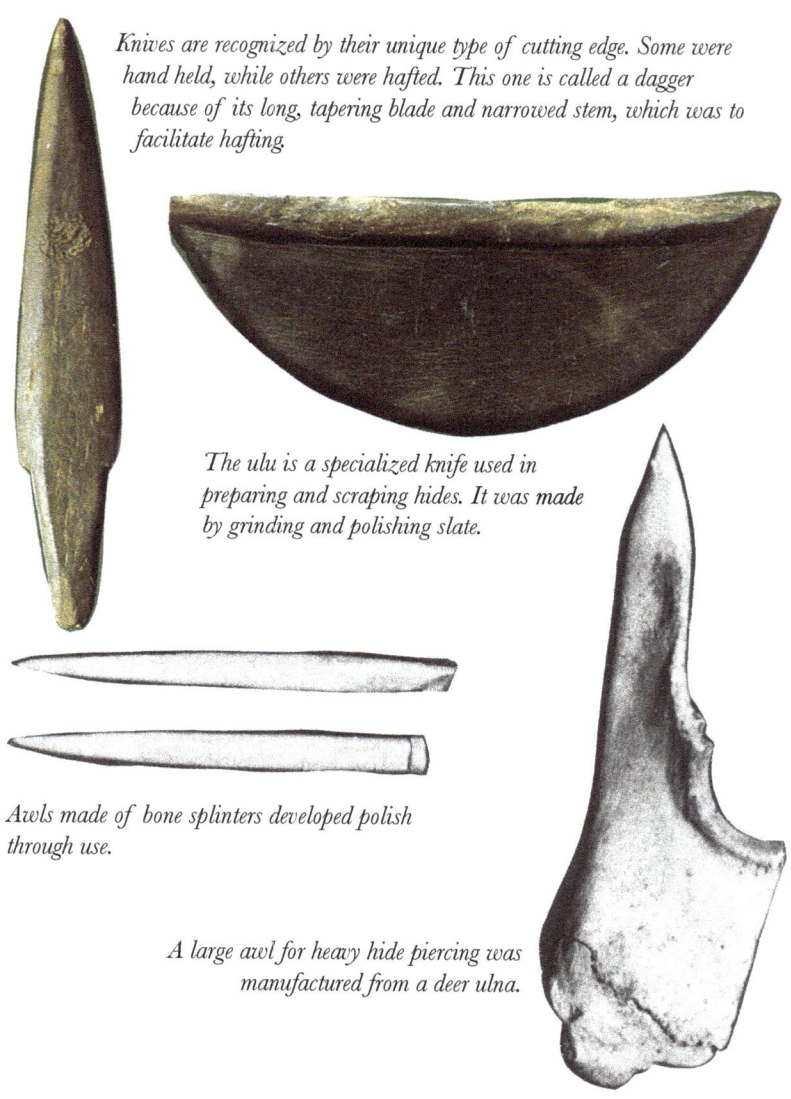

Knives are recognized by their unique type of cutting edge. Some were hand held, while others were hafted. This one is called a dagger because of its long, tapering blade and narrowed stem, which was to facilitate hafting.

The ulu is a specialized knife used in preparing and scraping hides. It was made by grinding and polishing slate.

Awls made of bone splinters developed polish through use.

A large awl for heavy hide piercing was manufactured from a deer ulna.

The early peoples of the region used the bone awl for perforating hides. The high degree of polish found on this implement was caused by constant rubbing against the smooth hides. The point of the awl was maintained by abrasion on a whetstone. This was similar to the modern whetstone but had a groove to accommodate the tapering, cylindrical awl.

Another important article in the tool kit was the sinewstone. This was used to strip and stretch sinew for bow strings, lashing materials, lacrosse stick nets, and laces.

The Indigenous peoples' primary sources of raw materials were animals, plants and trees, and stones. Animal and plant materials were procured near their camps by hunting, fishing, and gathering. Although the people had been making their tools from high-quality flint found at quarries in the Hudson Valley for 10,000 years, this was not their only lithic source. They usually obtained a variety of useful stone for their tools from local stream and glacial deposits.

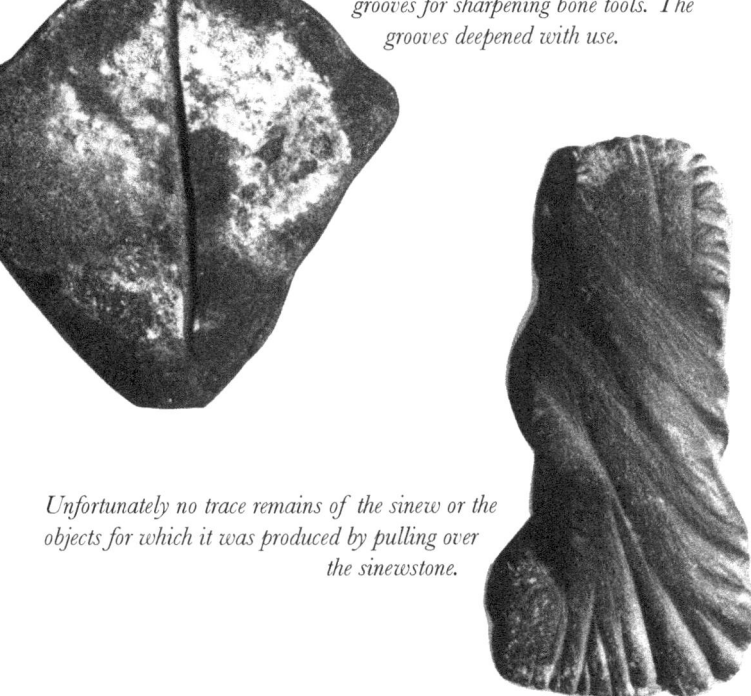

Whetstones were fine-grained stones with shallow grooves for sharpening bone tools. The grooves deepened with use.

Unfortunately no trace remains of the sinew or the objects for which it was produced by pulling over the sinewstone.

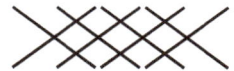

UTENSILS AND POTTERY

Steatite or soapstone was also quarried by the Indigenous peoples. Extensive quarries existed at one time in Portland, Litchfield, Torrington, and Bristol, Connecticut. Because the stone is so soft, it could be gouged out in large chunks with quarry picks. The raw soapstone pieces were then roughly shaped into vessels, such as bowls. These were used extensively before the development of ceramics.

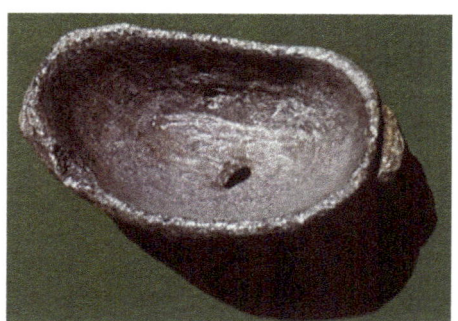

A completed steatite bowl has been ritually "killed" for inclusion with a burial. The hole in the bottom is to release the spirit to accompany the deceased.

Quarry picks for soapstone working were long and relatively narrow finegrained stones. The working end is smoothed through use.

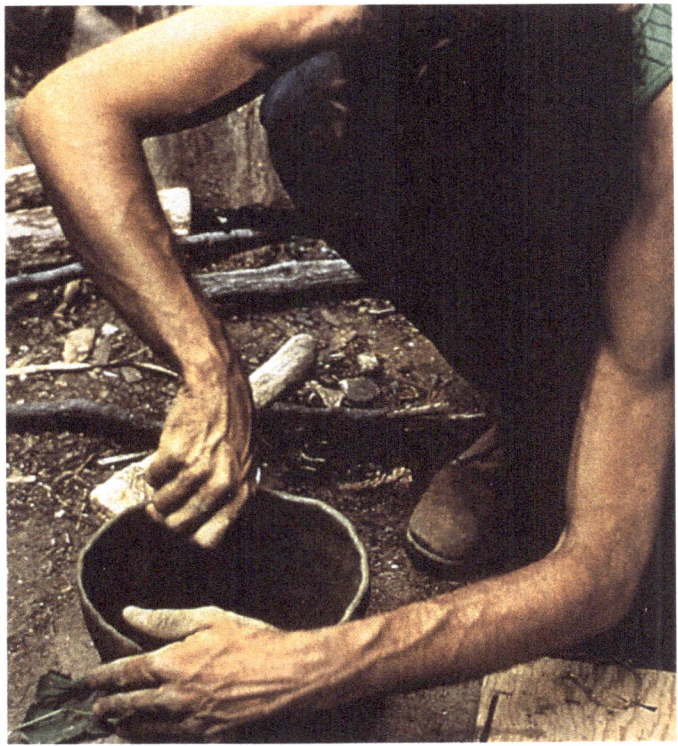

The pot is carefully shaped and smoothed prior to air drying and then firing.

The manufacture of pottery, using clay mixed with temper or grog (crushed shell, stone, gravel, steatite, or fibers), represents the first instance of a chemical reaction being used to make utensils in the New World. The pottery bowl was first shaped by working wet clay using either the coiling technique or the pinching technique. Coiling was accomplished by making long, cylindrical strips of clay that were then connected and coiled, one upon another, to give shape to the walls of the pot. To use the pinching technique to make a bowl, the potter started with a ball of clay, then worked it to leave a depression in the center. By slowly pulling and pinching the clay up from the center, the potter shaped the walls of the pot, which were then paddled with special tools to remove air bubbles.

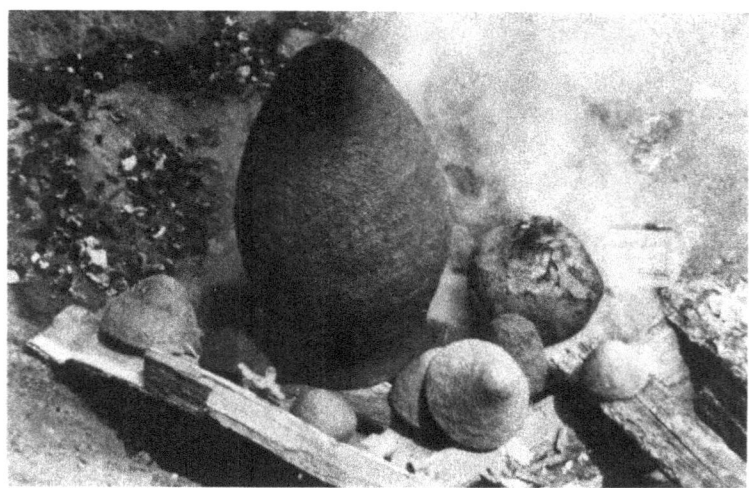

The pots have to be slowly heated and slowly cooled, lest they shatter.

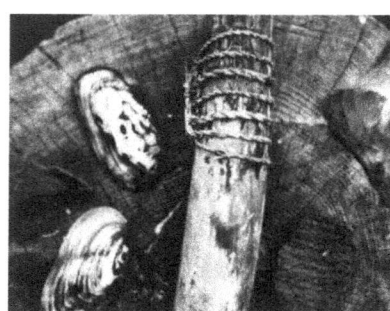

Surface decoration was applied by a cord-wrapped paddle, shells, and sharp stones, among other implements.

Surface decoration was usually applied at this stage by making impressions or by cutting into the wet clay. The implements pictured were used to paddle and scrape the sides of the nearly finished vessel. After air drying, the pot was fired in an open pit. When the fire had died out, the pot was carefully removed and allowed to cool slowly in order to prevent cracking.

The Indigenous peoples of New England did not use a potter's wheel, slips, glazes, or handles in the manufacture or design of their vessels. Coloring came from the clay and temper used, rather than from paint.

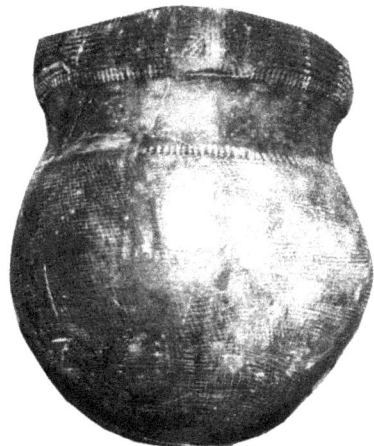

Careful cord-wrapped stick impressions form horizontal, slanted, and vertical lines on the collar and rim.

Most of the decoration on this vessel is from the cord-wrapped stick paddling the body and impressing the collar and lip.

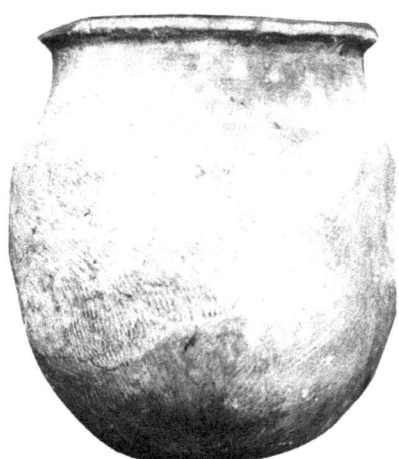

THE HISTORIC PERIOD

T o complete the history of the New England Indigenous peoples, the archaeologist must study pre-Contact artifacts in relation to those made in the Historic period. Although European influence spread quickly and devastatingly, curiosity and an interest in novelty inspired a few people to record some of the items of Indigenous culture. No detailed records or inventories are known, but a few specific items were described and have been preserved in the written record. The descriptions of these artifacts have been used to create the modern facsimiles shown in the following photographs.

A simple rattle was made by placing pebbles into a bark pouch wrapped around a wooden handle.

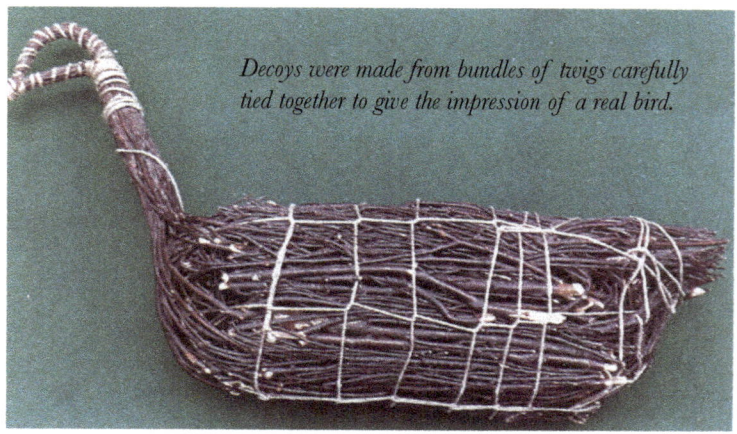

Decoys were made from bundles of twigs carefully tied together to give the impression of a real bird.

Rattles were used in religious and social ceremonies. The depiction or use of animal parts in their manufacture and design added significance to the ceremony. Bird and animal decoys were used as they are still used today.

Many different forms of baskets were made. Although the precise nature of prehistoric basketry is unknown for New England, the form illustrated was made using resources and technology that would have been available to pre-Contact Indigenous peoples. However, the final design and form may have been influenced by European styles.

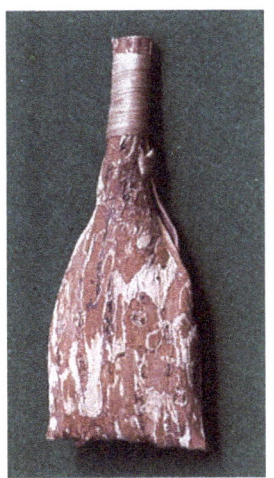

This rattle was made from a snapping turtle.

Mukoks are decorated by using natural dyes or by carefully cutting away the upper layer of bark to reveal the lighter area underneath.

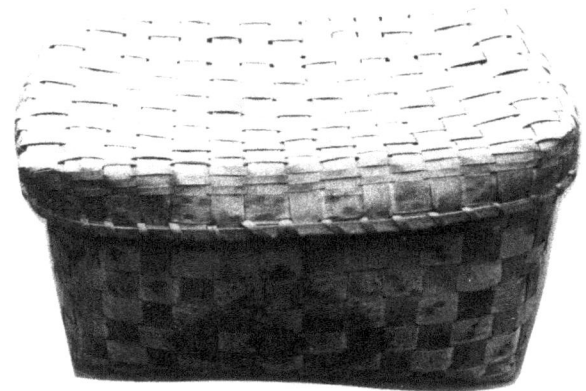

Baskets were made from thin wooden splints. The decoration on this one was applied by a block stamp dipped into a natural dye.

For wearing during the winter, summer moccasins were lined with woven cornhusks.

The *'mukok'*, or bark basket, was decorated by removing layers of the bark in one area and not in others. The mukok was laced together with a split twig and the seams were caulked with pitch. Tree resin would have been a readily available substitute.

Moccasins were made from deer hide. Elaborate decorative motifs using porcupine-quill or moosehair embroidery and soft colors from natural dyes were reserved for moccasins worn on special occasions. Designs that were done with glass beads obtained in trade with Europeans incorporate both traditional and European designs.

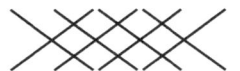

DATING

Carbon-14 is the most widely used technique for dating prehistoric Indigenous artifacts. The samples collected from an excavation are sent to a laboratory for analysis. Organic materials, such as shell, bone, charcoal, wood, or plant fibers, can be dated using this method, provided they date from a few hundred to 75,000 years ago.

Certain kinds and styles of artifacts are found over a very wide area and are dated to a specific period of time using the carbon-14 method. Thus, when a specific style of artifact is found, it can be dated on the basis of its similarity to other artifacts when it is found in a site that cannot be dated by carbon-14. For example, fluted points of the general Clovis type are consistently dated to about 10,000 years ago. Thus, if they are found outside of a datable context (i.e., no charcoal was with them), an archaeologist knows approximately how old they are by their physical traits alone.

Dating on the basis of style or similarity is not always entirely accurate, since certain styles reappeared at many different times through the ages. Therefore, stratigraphy is useful in providing a relative date.

Stratigraphy is a geological term that refers to the origin, composition, and arrangement of layers in the ground. If the layers have not been disturbed by previous digging, the earliest occupation of a given site will be the deepest one. As an area is covered with silt, debris from the first occupation is buried. As the site is reoccupied, each succeeding occupation leaves debris on the surface of the ground. When archaeologists dig the site, they will encounter the most recent artifacts first. Digging through the layers and noting the various artifacts found in each can reveal the sequence of occupations at a site. Although the specific age of each stratum is not known, this technique reveals the order in which they occurred.

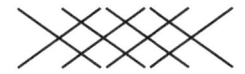

SUMMARY

The archaeological record of the Indigenous peoples of the Northeast began at least 10,000 years ago with the Paleo-American. Typical tools of that period were fluted points and stemmed drills, scrapers, and knives. At the beginning of the Archaic period, about 8,000 years ago, projectile point styles changed and the fluted point was replaced by various notched forms. The other tools of the Paleo-Americans were so essential to their daily existence that Archaic people continued to use them. Because of differences in preservation over time and changing subsistence patterns, we find fishhooks, net weights, harpoons, and other evidence of a more diverse food supply being pursued in the sites of the Archaic people. Axes, celts, and gouges provide evidence that woodworking was being practiced at this time. The Woodland period began about 3,000 years ago with the advent of ceramics, domesticated plants and animals, and smoking pipes. From this period come the best-preserved organic materials that have been found at prehistoric sites.

The Contact period began with the arrival of the Europeans. Prior to this time, the story of the Indigenous peoples of the Northeast was one of very gradual change, but in the period of European contact, Indigenous culture, economy, technology, and ideology changed very rapidly. Little remained of traditional tools or subsistence techniques, except a fragmentary written record. The archaeological record is important in supplementing the written history of the pre-Contact Indigenous peoples in the Northeast.

other indigenous culture titles from HANCOCK HOUSE PUBLISHERS

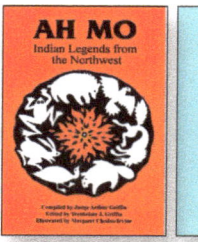

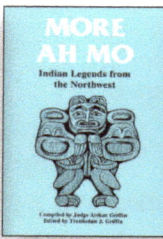

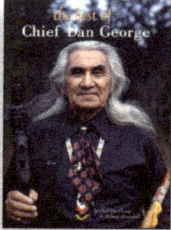

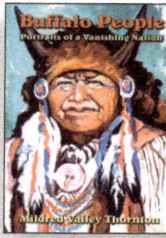

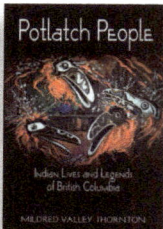

Ah Mo
Tren Griffin
978-0-88839-244-2
5½ x 8½, sc, 64 pp
$7.95

More Ah Mo
Tren Griffin
978-0-88839-303-6
5½ x 8½, sc, 64 pp
$7.95

The Best of Chief Dan George
978-0-88839-544-3
5½ x 8½, sc, 216 pp
$9.95

Buffalo People
Mildred Thornton
978-0-88839-479-8
5½ x 8½, sc, 208 pp
$24.95

Potlatch People
Mildred Thornton
978-0-88839-491-0
5½ x 8½, sc, 320pp
$24.95

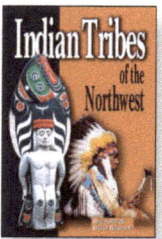

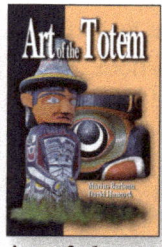

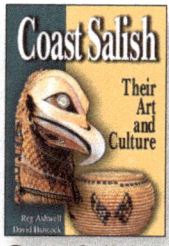

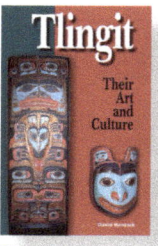

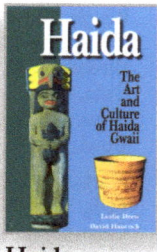

Indian Tribes
*Reg Ashwell
David Hancock*
978-0-88839-619-8
full color, 5½ x 8½
sc, 96 pp
$11.95

Art of the Totem
*Marius Barbeau
David Hancock*
978-0-88839-618-1
5½ x 8½ sc, 64pp
$9.95

Coast Salish
*Reg Ashwell
David Hancock*
978-0-88839-620-4
full color, 5½ x 8½
sc, 96 pp
$11.95

Tlingit
David Hancock
978-0-88839-530-2
5½ x 8½, sc, 96 pp
$12.95

Haida
*Leslie Drew,
David Hancock*
978-0-88839-621-X
full color 5½ x 8½
sc, 96 pp
$12.95

We-gyet Wanders On
Kitanmax School
978-0-88839-636-5
8½ x 11, sc, 72 pp
$14.95

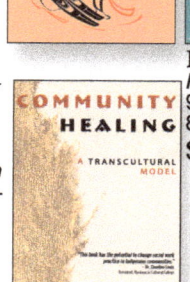

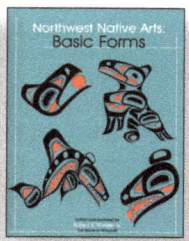

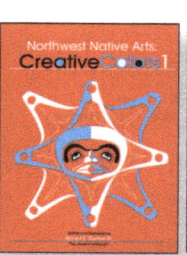

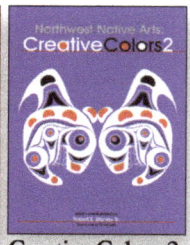

Community Healing: *a transcultural model*
Geneva Ensign
978-0-888390-578
5½ x 8½, sc, 280 pp
$29.95

Basic Forms
Robert E. Stanley Sr.
978-0-88839-506-1
8½ x 11, sc, 64 pp
$11.95

Creative Colors 1
Robert E. Stanley Sr.
978-0-88839-532-0
8½ x 11, sc, 32 pp
$6.95

Creative Colors 2
Robert E. Stanley Sr.
978-0-88839-533-7
8½ x 11, sc, 24 pp
$5.95

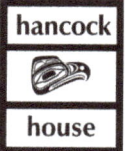

Hancock House Publishers
19313 0 Ave, Surrey, BC V3Z 9R9
www.hancockhouse.com
sales@hancockhouse.com
1-800-938-1114